Insight Text Guide

Therese O'Haire

Blade Runner

Dir. Ridley Scott

insight

First published in 2001, reprinted with revisions in 2013.

Insight Publications Pty Ltd
89 Wellington Street
St Kilda VIC 3182
Australia
Tel: +61 3 9523 0044
Fax: +61 3 9523 2044
Email: books@insightpublications.com.au

www.insightpublications.com.au

ISBN: 9781875882304

Insight Publications is committed to environmentally responsible production practices. This book has been printed on sustainably manufactured paper in Australia to minimise our carbon footprint and support local industries and expertise.

Printed in Australia.

contents

CHARACTER MAP

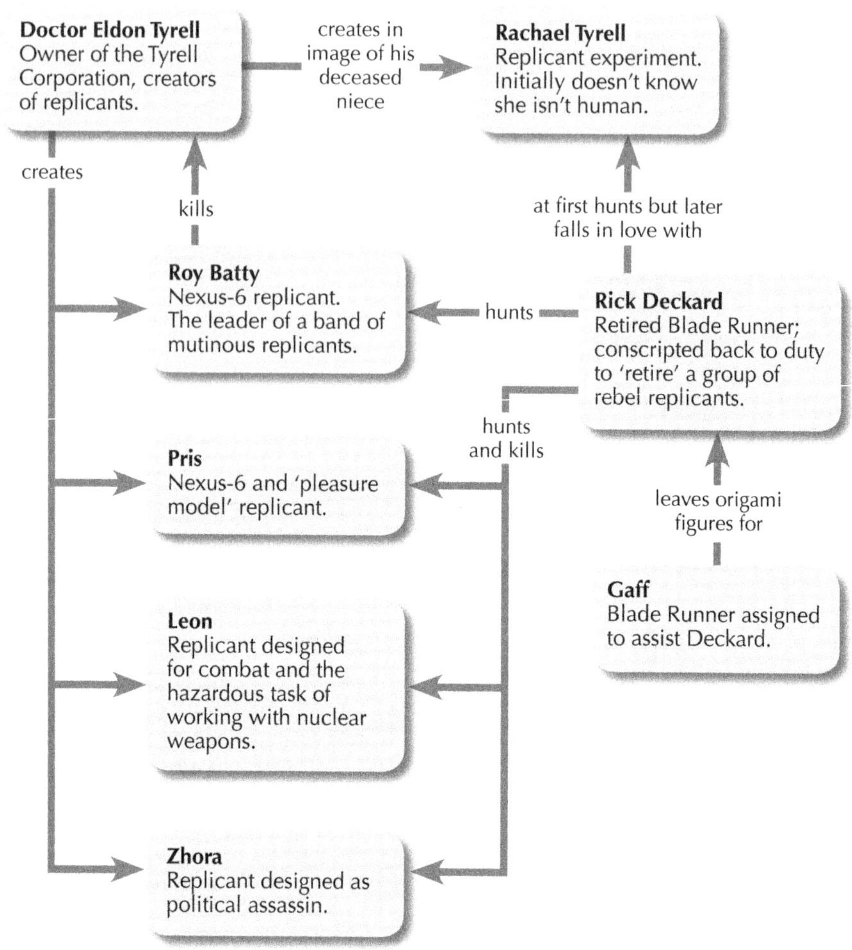

OVERVIEW

On the surface, *Blade Runner* appears to be a sombre, rather slow-moving mix of detective thriller and science fiction movie, shot in film noir style. But a deeper study of the film reveals layers of meaning beneath the gloomy, crowded sets, the sometimes sketchily drawn characters and the meandering storyline. The film raises disturbing questions, the most important of which is 'What does it mean to be human?' *Blade Runner* deals with fascinating ideas and is so dense, both visually and thematically, that it provides scope for almost endless discussion and writing. Because of this, it has become a movie classic.

About the director

Ridley Scott was born in England and attended the Royal College of Art in London. He worked as a set designer and director in British television, going on to direct more than 2000 television commercials for his own company. His attention to visual stylisation in his commercials, including distinctive atmospheric lighting effects, continued into the feature films that he began directing in 1977. His first was *The Duellists*, set in Napoleonic France, which won the best first-feature award at the Cannes Film Festival. His next three films were fantasies: *Alien* (1979), a science fiction horror story; *Blade Runner* (1982; recut 1992); and *Legend* (1985), an allegorical fairy tale.

Scott's next films were set in contemporary times, including the thrillers *Someone to Watch Over Me* (1987) and *Black Rain* (1989); again these were admired for their visual styling. While Scott's settings in *Thelma and Louise* (1991) were no less notable, the film's lead characters and feminist theme were the focus of critical attention. His *1492: Conquest of Paradise* (1992) was less well received. Other well-known films directed by Ridley Scott include *G.I. Jane* (1997), *Gladiator* (2000), *Black Hawk Down* (2001), *American Gangster* (2007) and *Robin Hood* (2010).

Synopsis

The opening 'crawl' to the film reads:

> Early in the 21st century, THE TYRELL CORPORATION advanced Robot evolution into the NEXUS phase – a being virtually identical to a human – known as a replicant.
>
> The Nexus-6 Replicants were superior in strength and agility, and at least equal in intelligence, to the genetic engineers who created them. Replicants were used Off-world as slave labour, in the hazardous exploration and colonization of other planets.
>
> After a bloody mutiny by a Nexus-6 combat team in an Off-world colony, Replicants were declared illegal on earth – under penalty of death.
>
> Special police squads – BLADE RUNNER UNITS – had orders to shoot to kill, upon detection, any trespassing Replicants.
>
> This was not called execution.
>
> It was called retirement.

Los Angeles, November 2019. The ominous, thudding rush of the soundtrack draws us into the world of *Blade Runner*. Explosions of gas and smoke belch from tall chimneys, which tower over an immense industrial wasteland. A blue flash of lightning streaks through the sky above a carpet of tiny lights. Through this, a wasp-like Spinner buzzes towards twin monoliths of stone and glass and, for a brief moment, the flame of an explosion is reflected in the iris of a blue-grey eye; its expression is fixed, staring, emotionless.

Los Angeles in 2019 is a crowded and decaying civilisation. Whether due to global warming or to the effects of 'World War Terminus' – as Philip K. Dick suggested in the novel from which *Blade Runner* was adapted – we are introduced to a society that has become a nonsensical mix of urban grunge and high technology; street food-stalls and flying vehicles; neon lights and steamy acid rain.

Technology has provided an answer to Earth's problems. Those who are smart enough, brave enough or able enough have left Earth to establish colonies 'Off-world' on other planets. The giant Tyrell Corporation has created 'replicants', android slaves who appear almost identical to humans. They do what slaves have always done: the tasks too menial, arduous or degrading for their 'superiors' – the humans – to do.

The development of the superior Nexus-6 model has created a further problem, however. Some of these replicants have mutinied and returned to Earth for reasons of their own. On Earth, their physical and/or mental superiority as well as their desire to challenge their creators has led to the development of an elite group of police whose sole purpose is to hunt down and 'retire' these runaway replicants.

Enter the main character of this film. Rick Deckard, a cop recruited to the ranks of the Blade Runners, has just resigned from the force, and we see him sitting amongst the multi-cultural mayhem of Los Angeles' mean streets, reading a newspaper.

With the appearance of the sinister Gaff, Deckard is whisked back to police headquarters, which is just as seedy, hectic and under-resourced as any we might see on a present day police drama. He is given little choice but to return to duty. He has been called to retire four replicants, contemptuously called 'skin jobs' by Inspector Bryant, whose hearty joviality only thinly disguises his threat that Deckard, should he refuse, could easily become one of the 'little people'.

Throughout the course of his 'search and destroy' mission, we begin to see signs of the doubt and confusion that may have caused Deckard to resign in the first place. He forms an uncharacteristically passionate and protective attachment to Rachael Tyrell, a Nexus-6 replicant who believes she is human. He also finds himself becoming more and more uncomfortable with his role as a Blade Runner: he can no longer kill cold-bloodedly, but rather finds himself pitying the plight of these 'perfect' beings that have so little control over any aspect of their lives.

The film reaches its climax in the penultimate scene where Deckard, the best that humanity has to offer, meets technology's best in Roy Batty, the leader of the rebel replicants. Their desperate battle ends with Roy's surprising about-face as his own programmed 'natural' death approaches. He saves Deckard's life, then attempts to communicate to him something of the beauty and mystery of his Off-world experience, before accepting his death with dignified resignation.

Deckard, deeply affected by this emotionally charged scene, races back to his apartment, where he finds Rachael – unharmed although Gaff has been there. They are both now outlaws: Rachael because society does not recognise her humanity and Deckard because he has rediscovered his. As outlaws, their future must be uncertain at best. The film ends as the elevator doors close on them, symbolising the beginning of a new and limited life. Gaff's words set out the parameters: 'Too bad she won't live. But then again, who does?'

BACKGROUND & CONTEXT

Blade Runner, adapted from the science fiction novel *Do Androids Dream of Electric Sheep?* by Philip K. Dick, had its first cinema release in 1982. It cost $28 million, featured popular star Harrison Ford and was directed by the highly regarded Ridley Scott – and it flopped. It was both a financial and a critical failure. The film was described by critics as dour, downbeat and slow-moving. They were quick to point out mistakes in continuity and complained about what they saw as a meandering storyline, suggesting a better title might have been *Blade Crawler.* The public's reaction was equally lukewarm. Gross box office takings for this release were only $14 million.

It might have been expected that the film would descend into video store oblivion. Instead the reverse happened – it garnered a strong cult following. Seeing it at home on video, people were able to revisit the teeming world of *Blade Runner* to investigate its murky depths in detail – and they did. *Blade Runner* became a rental champion. *Cityspeak,* a fan magazine (now fanzine on the internet) dedicated solely to *Blade Runner,* was published semi-regularly throughout the 1980s. *Retrofitting Blade Runner,* an entire book comprised of scholarly essays on the film, appeared in 1991.

When you look at *Blade Runner* you will see how home viewing on the small screen or in a small group might be better than cinema viewing. While *Blade Runner* has some exhilarating action that would look stunning on the big screen, the real action that pertains to the main themes of this movie is mostly in the small things – subtle hints rather than statements, clues half hidden in the gloom, the monotonous background itself. These come through more strongly, perhaps, on the small screen, where the big action is reduced in physical size and thus becomes much less shocking and attention-diverting as a consequence. These hints and clues necessitate more than one viewing of *Blade Runner* to fully grasp and appreciate their significance. In addition, *Blade Runner* was shot using the devices usually associated with television production, with a small cast, many close-ups, basic plot, and simple sets, action, lighting, and sound. The director's background in television commercials is worth taking into consideration in this respect.

This movie's video renaissance prompted the release of *Blade Runner – The Director's Cut* in 1992. This version was different from the original in some interesting ways and spawned yet another flurry of dissection and discussion amongst ardent fans. The growth of the internet provided fans with a new medium for communication; there are now hundreds of sites dedicated to the critical reassessment and celebration of this one motion picture.

So what is it about this movie that has inspired such fanatical interest? Certainly, the amazing production design and elaborately detailed sets are intriguing, but it is the characters and ideas in *Blade Runner* that draw viewers back to it time and time again. This text raises questions about what it is to be human, confronting its characters (and its audiences) with excruciating moral dilemmas. In the words of Rick Deckard's discarded voice-over, this film asks the questions we all want answered, 'Where did I come from? Where am I going? How long have I got?'

Blade Runner deals with fascinating ideas and is so dense both visually and thematically that it provides scope for almost endless original discussion and writing. These qualities contributed to an unpromising start in 1982, but they have endured to make the picture a movie classic.

GENRE & SETTING

Blade Runner has been labelled 'Future Noir', a blend of two quite distinct film genres, science fiction and film noir. It is worth taking a brief look at the features of each of these and how *Blade Runner* sits between them.

Science fiction

Science fiction literature and films deal with the impact of actual or imagined science upon society or individuals. They ask the question, 'What if a scientific development is taken to its logical conclusion?' They also tend to address the anxieties we all have about current social, scientific or technological trends. If you trace the history of science fiction novels and films, you can clearly see in *Blade Runner* some of the concerns underlying them, such as invasion, infiltration by the forces of evil, the fear of robots and questions of identity and humanity.

In this case, the novel on which *Blade Runner* was based, *Do Androids Dream of Electric Sheep?*, was written during the Vietnam War and reflected its author's concerns about the dehumanising effect of 'fighting the good fight'. The world he created was ruled by the scientific bureaucracy that had taken technology and ruthless utilitarianism to their extremes. In *Blade Runner*, Ridley Scott has the human (is he really?) Rick Deckard question his own humanity, both physically and morally, while the replicant, Roy Batty, claims his as he meets his own maker.

Film noir

This genre of film arose in the US during the 1940s, perhaps influenced by the fear of Communism that pervaded the country at the time. Film noir movies paint a picture of a world that is dark, seedy and in moral decay. The style is gloomy, shadowy and cramped.

The typical plot follows the adventures of a lone, world-weary cop or private investigator living on the murky border between polite society and its criminal counterpart. This detective (traditionally male) is the protector of society, cynical in the extreme but with a moral edge, probably drinks too much, attracts women, and often has a penchant for explaining himself to the viewer in deadpan voice-overs. An apparently routine case becomes both mysterious and dangerous, involving him with villainous characters and, particularly, with a *femme fatale* who seduces the hero but is thwarted in her plans to murder him. He becomes entangled in a situation where he must make a moral decision: will he stay true to his principles or fall prey to the glamorous seductress? In the end, the film noir rules demand that 'morality' wins out while the *femme fatale* pays for her immoral ways.

Rick Deckard has all the trappings of a film noir hero, although he loses his deadpan voice-over in *The Director's Cut*. The storyline too follows a traditional path, with mysterious clues, damsels in distress and the usual assortment of weird and wonderful characters. Ridley Scott plays with our expectations of this genre, but refuses to end his film in the standard way.

Setting and visual style

The production design of *Blade Runner* has always been one of the most celebrated aspects of the film. Ridley Scott's training as a set designer is evident in many of his films, none more so than this. His production style involves what might be called 'visual layering'; he insists on the development of sets, props, costumes, soundtrack and atmosphere that is equivalent to rock music's 'wall of sound'. This is done in an effort to create a richly textured and wholly believable setting for the narrative.

In *Blade Runner*, Scott achieves his masterpiece; Los Angeles in 2019 is a dark, teeming and alienating megalopolis in which the Blade Runner and Tyrell's replicants can move convincingly. The viewer is carried effortlessly into the bleak, crumbling world of the director's dystopic vision.

You should make sure that you can distinguish all of the components of this complex 'layering' technique. Apart from the crowding of his sets,

Scott also uses elements such as:

- all-pervading acid rain, suggesting ecological mismanagement
- steam or mist
- intrusive shafts of light and bursts of flame
- large, slowly turning fan blades
- cramped interior sets
- ever-present blimps bombarding the citizens with advertising
- a wild ethnic mix of extras
- moody music
- sounds appropriate to the action but out of place in the environment.

Some of the scenes you might like to examine for examples of this layering are:

- Scene 4 – our extraordinary first glimpse of the Blade Runner's world
- Scene 10 – Chew's Ice House
- Scene 13 – the decaying Bradbury building; J.F.'s apartment
- Scene 14 – Deckard's apartment
- Scene 17 – the Snake Pit nightclub; the chase
- Scene 22 – Tyrell's room
- Scene 25 – the rooftop.

You should devote at least one viewing of *Blade Runner* to noting these and other aspects that add to the visual and auditory richness of this text. Consider how much the medium of film allows the director to convey to the audience compared with what can be conveyed by the printed word and conversely how much it allows to remain unsaid. You should take note of the following:

- how the soundtrack assists in creating the confusion of the L.A. streetscape
- how and why the music varies from frantic, synthetic sound to nostalgic, gentle piano

- how the director uses long-shots to create a sense of scale or physical action, and close-ups to explore psychological or mental action
- how special photographic effects and dream sequences are used
- how lighting is used, e.g. to create the eerie darkness of an earth with little sunlight, or the atmosphere of the cavernous Tyrell building as Rachael takes the Voigt-Kampff test
- how costuming assists in the creation of character, e.g. contrast Rachael and Zhora's costuming; Deckard and Gaff's
- whose point of view we take throughout the narrative – do we see through the eyes of Deckard? Rachael? Roy? Anyone?
- how characters have been created by the choice of actor, e.g. Rutger Hauer as the beautiful but sinister Nexus-6; Sean Young as the elegant, pompadoured and tragic Rachael; Edward James Olmos as the chilling, threatening Gaff.

SCENE-BY-SCENE ANALYSIS

This analysis includes some commentary and suggested ideas you might like to explore during your 'readings' of the film. The best way to tease out your ideas and understandings is, of course, to discuss them with others.

Scene 1 – Introduction to the plot

The opening 'crawl' sets the scene giving an abstract of the story and the location of the film. It is essential that you understand who the replicants are and what their function is. It is not explained why they have suddenly begun to mutiny or why the decision has been made to kill them on sight. What threat might they pose?

Scene 2 – L.A. 2019 from the air

Los Angeles 2019, as described in the Synopsis. This scene is only brief, but its visual styling sets the mood; ominous and alienating. There seem to be two distinct levels in this society; the masses at ground level and the scientific bureaucrats high in their pyramid-like fortresses. The huge staring eye is the first of many references to eyes throughout the text. What might be suggested by its glassy, emotionless stare?

Scene 3 – Leon takes the Voigt-Kampff test

Leon Kowalski: Engineer, waste disposal, a new employee of the Tyrell Corporation, sits for a Voigt-Kampff test, a series of questions designed to provoke an emotional response, with pupil dilation being the measure of that response. Leon seems agitated, uncomfortable, continually interrupting Mr Holden's questioning to establish the ground rules for the test. When asked to describe the good things about his mother, Leon shoots Holden with a handgun he is holding underneath the table. The shots hurl Holden through the wall.

Are there any clues here that Leon is a replicant? Can you notice his faintly glowing eyes? Scott uses this as a signal to the audience that a character is a replicant – watch out for it in later scenes. Why does Leon react so violently to the question about his mother?

The Voigt-Kampff test is very significant. A little like a Lie Detector, the machine is an eye scanner (the eye again) which measures involuntary physical responses to emotional triggers, specifically pupil dilation. As replicants don't have emotions, their responses will differ from normal human responses.

The complicating factor here is that the Nexus-6 replicants are developing their own emotions, which makes it nearly impossible for them to be detected in this way. This is why Bryant and Deckard are so concerned when Deckard takes the machine to test it at the Tyrell Corporation. If the V-K machine no longer works, how will they be able to identify replicants at all? What will happen when humans can no longer be reliably distinguished from non-humans?

Scene 4 – We meet Deckard; Gaff 'arrests' him

A Los Angeles street, showing the incredible lengths Scott went to in order to establish a convincing setting. Lower-class citizens of all racial origins swarm in the confined space. It is dark, crowded and steamy; acid rain drips constantly. Rick Deckard sits reading the employment pages of a newspaper as he waits for food ordered from a noodle bar.

Gaff appears, speaking a patois that Deckard appears not to understand. This is Cityspeak, a mixture of Japanese, Spanish, German and guttertalk. Deckard is 'under arrest' and is taken to Inspector Bryant, to a building that, on the outside at least, resembles the Battle Star from *Star Wars*. Inside it looks like a scene from any 1990s police drama. Bryant knows Deckard well and greets him in an almost apologetic, ingratiating manner. This quickly gives way to not-so-veiled threats when Deckard seems reluctant to return to duty. Deckard eventually capitulates; he has no choice it seems.

Deckard, a human, seems to have little control over his life. What does this mean in relation to the question of who is human and who is a non-human slave? What does Bryant mean by his threat about 'little people'? What is his attitude to the replicants?

Scene 5 – Bryant assigns Deckard his task

Bryant and Deckard watch the video of Leon's V-K test. Leon's final words continue to repeat in Deckard's mind. Why? The mutineers have tried to break in to the Tyrell building. Why? This scene sets up the mystery of the replicants' return and establishes Deckard's task at the same time. The replicants are introduced by way of 'incept tapes', represented much as models of bikes or computers might be – description, function, expected life span.

The central problem of the almost-human androids is introduced, along with the cynical solution – a four-year life span, so that their fledgling emotions have no time to develop fully and cause problems. Deckard is sent to try out the Voigt-Kampff machine on a replicant at the Tyrell Corporation. Gaff leaves a tiny origami figure of a chicken on Bryant's desk. This action sets up a pattern present throughout the film, where Gaff leaves these tiny figures as messages for others or comments on Deckard's state of mind.

Note here the cosy relationship between Tyrell and the Police Department. What might that mean about the power structure in 2019? Who is in charge? What might that mean for the ordinary citizen?

This scene introduces one of the most talked-about anomalies of the film. Bryant says that *six* replicants had escaped and that *one* had been 'fried', leaving *five*. We know that Deckard only kills *four* replicants. Some fans suggest that this means Deckard may be the sixth replicant, reprogrammed to believe he is human and forced to kill his own kind. The answer is far simpler: Scott removed scenes involving the sixth replicant, Mary, as a cost-cutting measure. This mistake in continuity was never remedied as a re-shoot would have been too expensive.

Scene 6 – Rachael takes the Voigt-Kampff test

In a cavernous room of the pyramid-like Tyrell building, Deckard meets Rachael, Tyrell's niece. She is such a contrast to what we already know of his world: she wears angular, forties-influenced clothes and a pompadour hairstyle. Her style is manicured and perfectly groomed, her lips shaped into an exaggerated Cupid's bow – the perfect *femme fatale*. Might she be someone's idea of the perfect woman? Whose?

An artificial owl flies through the cavernous room. Real animals are scarce and very valuable in this inhospitable world. Rachael immediately aligns herself with the corporation: 'our work'. She asks a very significant question, 'Have you ever retired a human by mistake?' Why does she ask this?

Then we meet Doctor Eldon Tyrell, the master genetic engineer. He wears an old-fashioned suit, a hand-tied bow tie and thick glasses. When he can create perfect beings, why does he have poor sight? Tyrell tricks Deckard into trying the test on Rachael. The camera focuses on her eyes: her irises are huge, luminous and opaque. The test goes on for a long time. Her attitude towards it is quite arrogant; she taunts Deckard with patronising comments about the intention of the questions. Finally her inappropriate response to the question about boiled dog shows her to be a replicant – they can learn the appropriate verbal response but cannot hide their emotional responses, or lack of them.

Tyrell sends Rachael out of the room. Deckard is outraged: 'How can it not know what it is?' Rachael believes she is human; she has been given false memory implants taken from Tyrell's real niece. Tyrell coolly explains that Rachael is 'an experiment, nothing more' and that this has been done as a measure of control; implanted memories give restless replicants a 'pillow for their emotions' and make them easier to control. This cynical idea seems to upset our hard-bitten hero. Why?

Scene 7 – Deckard and Gaff track Leon down

Back in the Spinner, Deckard and Gaff replay the video of Leon's V-K test to obtain the address of his hotel, 1187 Hunterwasser Street.

Scene 8 – Deckard finds the scale and photos

Down below in the 'real' world it is still raining. Deckard is taken to Leon's hotel. He retrieves a small, scale-like object from the bath and photographs from a chest of drawers – Leon's 'memories'? Gaff leaves behind a tiny origami figure of a matchstick man with a huge erection. Why?

Scene 9 – Roy and Leon on the street

Leon meets Roy outside a phone booth. Roy reports that he could not retrieve his 'precious photos' because a police officer was there. He seems bereft. Roy is annoyed, probably because the replicants have now lost their 'safe house' and they are all in jeopardy. Note that he does not berate Leon for his dangerous outburst. What might this suggest about their relationship?

Scene 10 – Chew's Ice House

Roy Batty and Leon walk the mean streets. Roy is the epitome of menace with his bleached-blonde hair, red-rimmed eyes and upturned Nazi-inspired collar. In this scene, we are given the first indication that Roy knows he is dying. His hand forms itself into a claw, the fingernails discoloured. He says, 'Time. Enough.' We are not sure whether this is a question or a statement.

He and Leon visit Chew, an eccentric genetic engineer who creates the Nexus-6 eyes in a freezing and incongruously decrepit setting. Roy makes awful 'eye' jokes, 'If only you could see what I've seen with your eyes.' Leon demonstrates his non-human status by putting his hand in a container of some viscous material we assume to be at sub-zero temperature. Roy's unnerving and inappropriate humour is quite disturbing for the viewer, as the replicants play with a terrified and rapidly freezing Chew. Why do you think Ridley Scott has the actors play the scene this way?

Chew is a direct link to the Tyrell Corporation and Roy wants to know, 'Morphology. Longevity. Incept dates.' Under threat, Chew sends them to J.F. Sebastian, another genetic engineer who may be able to help the replicants to get to Tyrell, 'Not an easy man to ... see ...'

A point of interest in this scene is the quotation Roy adapts from William Blake's prophetic poem *America*, which celebrates the American rebellion against King George:

> Fiery the angels fell,
> Deep thunder rolled around their shores,
> Burning with the fires of Orc.

This saves Roy from our assumption that he is just a menacing thug and establishes the idea that he has a real capacity for reflection and wonder. He's not a machine but a philosopher. He may also be seen as the 'fiery angel' falling from the skies to question his creator.

Scene 11 – Deckard drives home

Deckard drives home through a tunnel, again replaying the final lines of Leon's interview in his head. Why does this haunt him?

Scene 12 – Deckard confronts Rachael

Deckard arrives home, to the ninety-seventh floor of a building reminiscent of Gotham City. Rachael is waiting for him in the lift, startling Deckard (and us) with her sudden appearance. She wants to see him, but he only relents when she tells him that Tyrell won't see her. (Reminiscent of Roy's words in Scene 10. Is there a message here?)

She tries to prove her humanity with a photograph of her mother and herself. In perhaps the most emotionally wrenching moment of the film, Deckard brutally informs her that her memories are implants and that she is indeed a replicant. He even repeats the details of some of her most treasured childhood memories so that there can be no possible question.

Rachael becomes very upset; she is defenceless and pathetic, a great contrast to her aloof composure before the V-K test. In the face of her distress, Deckard backs down, says it was a joke and offers her a drink, but she leaves, throwing the now worthless photo to the floor. Deckard is left alone once again, looking at Rachael's and Leon's photographs.

Listen carefully during the close-up of Rachael's photograph. You can hear the faint sound of laughter and children playing, inserted in the soundtrack by Scott to create a sense of a real past connected to the photo.

You should think here about why Deckard is so deliberately callous towards Rachael. Why does he seem so angry? Notice, too, the infiltration of gentle piano music over the sirens and bells in the second half of the scene and the lonely mood as Deckard takes his drink out onto the balcony.

Scene 13 – Pris meets J.F.

Pris, sent by Roy, uses her Tyrell-given talents to manipulate her way into J.F. Sebastian's apartment. He is obviously lonely and cannot believe his luck; an easy target. The ominous music and Pris' change of expression are clues that this meeting does not bode well for Sebastian.

One question you might ask in this scene is, if the world of 2019 is so overpopulated, how can Sebastian live in the almost deserted Bradbury Building? This may be a carry-over from the book, where Philip K. Dick conceived the earth as a far emptier place. The Bradbury is an actual building in downtown L.A. Built in 1893, it was designed as the commercial building of the future. It is famous for its distinctive architecture and has been used as a location for many films and television features.

In the shooting of this scene, Daryl Hannah, who plays Pris, fractured her elbow in eight places when she careered into the window of J.F.'s 'armadillo car'.

Scene 14 – The unicorn scene

Deckard tries to reassure himself of his own human identity. He sits tinkling on the piano, itself a symbol of the past, surrounded by his 'proof' – sheet music and dozens of photographs of friends and relatives. Because he has lots of photos, more than Rachael or Leon, does that make his past more solid, more real? He is drunk and, as he slumps over the keys, we catch a glimpse of his memory, a pure white unicorn galloping in slow motion through a beautiful green forest.

How can we interpret this vision? If this is his memory, his proof of existence in a concrete past, and unicorns exist only in legend, then what of the rest of his memories? Perhaps only humans can have 'memories' not rooted in actual events. Ridley Scott is very interested in the ephemeral nature of memory as an anchor to identity. What makes us who we are? Do our memories define us? If not, then what does?

In sharp contrast to the languid, nostalgic mood of the first half of this scene, we now see Deckard use another photo, Leon's, to track down his quarry. The photo becomes a traitor again. Deckard is back in Blade Runner mode and he uses technology to help him. With the aid of the Esper, a voice-controlled super-computer linked to the Police Department, he enhances various sections of the photograph, effectively spying on the lifestyle of the replicants. Eventually, in the reflection of a mirror, he finds a scaly costume and behind it Zhora asleep on a couch in a remote and tiny section of the picture. She has a tattoo of a snake on her jaw line. Scale = snake? Notice the focus on Deckard's eyes in this scene. Are they luminous?

Scene 15 – The scale is identified

Deckard takes the scale to an old Cambodian 'peasant woman' for identification. She defies our assumptions (again things are not always as they seem) by showing herself to be an expert on artificial animals and using an electron microscope to ascertain the maker's serial number. It is an artificial snake scale. She sends Deckard to Abdul ben Hassan, an artificial animal manufacturer.

Scene 16 – Deckard and the snake maker

Deckard questions Abdul ben Hassan, who is at first reluctant to divulge any information, but capitulates in the face of Deckard's aggression. You might notice that the words spoken don't seem to match the actors' lip movements in this scene. They don't. The script was changed and new words recorded in post-production as the original dialogue was thought to be too confusing.

Scene 17 – Deckard finds and kills Zhora

Working from information given by the snake maker, Deckard goes to the Snake Pit, a crowded, smoky and decadent night club populated by slumming upper-class citizens. The owner, Taffey Lewis, is uncooperative, but provides Deckard with a lethal-looking drink, complete with worms. Zhora is performing an exotic dance as 'Miss Salome and the Snake'. As he waits, Deckard calls Rachael on the vid-phone and asks her to the bar for a drink. (How appropriate is this, given her 'background' and present situation?) She refuses.

When Zhora completes her act, he follows her to her dressing room, pretending to be an official from a show business organisation, there to prevent the exploitation of female performers. His nasal, whining voice and ingratiating manner are really quite funny, but not very convincing.

Zhora showers and dries her hair. (Notice the continuity error: her snake tattoo is missing.) Deckard maintains his role, but becomes distracted by her body. She gets the better of him by inviting him closer to 'Dry me'. She karate-chops him in the throat and begins to strangle him, but is interrupted and races out of the room.

He chases her ruthlessly, now again in Blade Runner mode. She is desperate, terrified, so vulnerable and exposed in her incongruous plastic outfit. (Note another continuity error in her footwear. The high-heeled boots she pulled on in the dressing-room have now become flat black running shoes.) Deckard shoots her twice in the back as she runs for her life and she crashes through several store windows. Finally she dies on the footpath in front of the mannequins, surrounded by jagged broken glass and garish neon. Just another doll. (Another distraction here is the fact that the stunt double in the chase looks very little like Joanna Cassidy.)

Scene 18 – 'Four more to go'

Deckard seems very disturbed by these events. He buys a bottle of Tsing Tao from a nearby stall. Gaff and Bryant arrive in a Spinner to tell him that there are 'four more to go'. When he demurs, they tell him that Rachael has run off and he must now kill her as well.

Scene 19 – Leon confronts Deckard

As he leaves to go home he catches a glimpse of Rachael in the background, but before he can do anything he is cornered by Leon, who violently interrogates him, playing with him as a cat might play with a mouse. He asks, 'Painful to live in fear, isn't it?' As Leon prepares to jab his fingers into Deckard's eyes and kill him, Rachael shoots him with Deckard's gun, which she has retrieved from the alleyway. How ironic it is that the Blade Runner is saved by a replicant who kills one of her own, especially as he has just been ordered to terminate her.

Scene 20 – The 'love scene'

Deckard and Rachael return to his apartment. They are both shaken. In one of the most memorable lines from the film, Rachael replies to Deckard's reassurance that the shakes are 'just part of the business' by saying, 'I'm not in the business – I *am* the business.' This underlines both her acceptance of her replicant status and her fear of what he might do. We realise that she has nowhere else to go; he is her last option.

Deckard agrees to let her go if she goes north, then she unwittingly echoes his own thoughts, 'Did you ever take that test yourself?' Why does she ask him this at this particular moment? Deckard collapses into sleep and Rachael sits at the piano, discovering that she can play. She plays the same sweet, romantic melody over which he had been brooding earlier. As she examines the photographs littering the piano, she lets her hair down; this makes her look far softer and more 'human', although her glowing, opaque eyes are very obvious here.

Deckard wakes and sits beside her. He tries to kiss her but she runs to the door. He grabs her roughly, manhandling her and insisting that she ask him to kiss her and to put his hands on her. The reason for this is not completely clear. Does Deckard order her around in an attempt to separate himself emotionally from this 'machine', or is he trying to convince her that her feelings are real, to show her that he can no longer think of her as a replicant? Is he trying to make her believe that he cares, or to prove it to himself? Why is he so insistent?

(Scott intended this 'love scene' to be rough, but how rough? There is an extraneous factor here; it is known that there was animosity between the two actors off set.)

Notice the lighting in this scene; it is very suggestive of film noir, with the light filtering in stripes through the blinds.

Scene 21 – Pris and Roy at J.F.'s apartment

Pris spray-paints a black mask over her eyes, which glow eerily red. You might like to discuss the significance of this. She and Sebastian talk. He tells her that he has a premature ageing disease, Methuselah Syndrome (a human with a limited life expectancy … just like a replicant?), and it is clear that she feels something for this paltry man whose time is also running out.

Roy arrives, having obviously been summoned by Pris, and the passion between the two is evident. He tells her of Leon's death and they talk like immature adolescents, with exaggerated facial expressions to match. Their emotions change like the wind; they have so little experience in handling such strong feelings. Even after Sebastian guesses that they are Nexus-6, they are able to seduce him with their offer of friendship and belonging; his genius does not make him immune to this most human of needs.

Scene 22 – Roy meets his maker

Roy and Sebastian manage to get into the Tyrell fortress with a masterly chess move, planned by Roy. At first, Roy is menacing and sinister, as is the soundtrack – 'It's not an easy thing to meet your maker.' This conversation may symbolise humanity's sometimes uneasy relationship with God.

Roy's eyes are hooded, opaque. He argues with Tyrell about possible remedies for his imminent death, again showing the extent of his own intellect. Tyrell convinces Roy there is no way of extending his life, then tries to have Roy accept his imminent demise by painting. 'The light that burns twice as bright burns half as long. And you have burned so very, very brightly, Roy …' says Tyrell. He tries to cast Roy in the role of biblical Prodigal Son, returning repentant to his forgiving and compassionate father – 'I've done questionable things.' Tyrell tries to prolong his own life by appealing to Roy's better instincts: ironic, considering he was deliberately created with none. Roy kisses Tyrell almost passionately on the mouth (like Judas?), then crushes his skull, pushing his thumbs into his eyes. Roy's face here shows sorrow, fury and pain. The owl turns an opaque, uncaring eye.

As Roy kills his 'father', does he kill hope, along with any human element of himself? Does he now become completely a machine? As we find out later, he also kills Sebastian, whom we last saw darting around helplessly looking for escape. As Roy stands in the lift, a shadow passes over his face and all we can see in him is determined and vengeful fury.

Scene 23 – Deckard heads for J.F.'s apartment

Deckard calls Sebastian's apartment from his car after hearing that Tyrell and Sebastian have been found dead. Pris' face appears fleetingly on the vid-phone screen, but she hangs up in alarm.

Scene 24 – Deckard retires Pris

Deckard prowls through Sebastian's toy-filled apartment. Pris is masquerading as a mannequin, her arms held stiffly and her head covered by a web-like veil. Discovered, she gets Deckard in a vice-like scissor grip. When he shoots her, she thrashes around on the ground at a speed that only a machine could maintain.

Scene 25 – Roy and Deckard play the Game of Life and Death

Roy returns to the apartment and shows real pain when he discovers Pris' body. He begins a cat-and-mouse game with Deckard; the hunter becomes the hunted. Roy catches Deckard, callously breaks two of his fingers as punishment for his killings so far, then releases him to give him a start in what will be a final race for life.

Roy fills the brief wait grieving over Pris. It is obvious that Roy's relentless but almost playful attitude stems from a disregard for his own life, which he knows must end very soon, and the complete assurance that he will catch and overcome Deckard. Deckard on the other hand clings tenaciously to his life in the belief that he has years to fight for. This scene is played out between the best that humanity is and the best that it can create. 'Aren't you the good man?' Roy asks Deckard.

Note the soundtrack during the pursuit.

Roy chases Deckard through the deserted building and up onto the rooftop. He punches his hand, and then his head through the wall, reminding us that, with his super-human strength, he could easily end Deckard's life at any time he chooses. Rather, he watches with fascination as the Blade Runner fights for his life; we even sense a degree of admiration in Roy's attitude here. When Roy's hand begins to seize up and die, he pushes a huge nail through his palm. Why does he do this?

Finally, Deckard jumps for his life over the chasm between two buildings, slips and clings on to a jutting beam, his tired and broken fingers threatening to give way at any moment. Roy watches, mesmerised, then at the last possible moment, grabs Deckard's wrist with his dying hand and hauls him up onto the roof. Deckard cowers away, but Roy simply sits cross-legged in front of him. Under the dark, dripping sky, Roy tries to communicate to Deckard some of the wonders he has seen – his emotional and philosophical response to the universe, to his short but precious life.

Deckard is moved by this insight and by such gracious acceptance of the inevitable. When Roy says, 'All those moments … will be lost … in time, like … tears … in rain. Time … to die', we are not sure whether it is raindrops or tears that we see on the tough Blade Runner's face. As Roy surrenders to death, sitting like a marble statue in the rain, he releases the dove he has been holding and it flies up into the mysteriously blue sky.

What might be the Blade Runner's thoughts during this sequence?

This scene has come under a great deal of criticism over the years. Some say that it simply goes on for too long and loses momentum; others focus on the Christian symbolism of the nail through the palm and the dove rising like a spirit into the heavens, considering it too heavy-handed.

Is the momentarily lighter sky symbolic of hope? (In fact, the dove couldn't or wouldn't fly away in the gloom of shooting; this section of the scene had to be shot during post-production in England.)

Despite these limitations, this scene is a very moving one. Rutger Hauer was so caught up by this time in the complex character of Roy that he composed the touching 'tears in rain' line.

Scene 26 – Gaff congratulates Deckard

As Deckard sits stunned and emotionally drained on the rooftop, we see a Spinner rise slowly in the background. Gaff emerges and delivers two enigmatic lines. He congratulates Deckard saying, 'You've done a man's job, sir.' Then, as he turns to leave, he comments, 'It's too bad she won't live. But then again, who does?' Deckard realises that Gaff's words mean he knows both where Rachael is and the nature of their relationship. Knowing Gaff, he fears that Rachael has been killed or is about to be.

Scene 27 – Deckard and Rachael leave town

A desperate Deckard arrives at his apartment to find the door open. He creeps in and finds Rachael in his bed, a sheet covering her head. He lifts the blanket, puts his cheek to hers and, as he realises she is warm and alive, we see a look of utter relief wash over his face. He asks her gently whether she loves and trusts him and this time there is no hesitation in her answers, only weariness. As they cautiously head for the lift, Rachael's shoe brushes something on the floor. Deckard picks it up to discover a tiny silver paper unicorn. He nods and seems almost to manage a wry smile in recognition of its meaning. They step into the lift and the doors close.

Much has been written about the interpretation of this final scene. What message is it that Gaff has left for Deckard? If the unicorn-memory was Deckard's, then how does Gaff know about it? Is the only possible conclusion that Deckard himself is a replicant and Gaff has access to his memory files?

If so, and Gaff has really been Deckard's 'minder' all along, then why does he let these two replicants go free?

If you make the conclusion right at the end of the film that Deckard is indeed a replicant, then how might that change your understanding of the major themes of the text, humanity and the nature of the difference between humankind and machines?

CHARACTERS & RELATIONSHIPS

Rick Deckard (Harrison Ford)

The Deckard we meet at the beginning of the film is a classically drawn film noir protagonist – world-weary, hard-bitten and trench-coated. He seems resigned to the alienation and cruelty of his world. The only clue that we are given that it is not quite so simple is that he has quit his job as a Blade Runner.

The character of Deckard soon breaks free from the two-dimensional shackles of the cynical and soulless detective. After he is conscripted back into service, we can see his discomfort: when Bryant tells him about the replicants' four-year life span; when Tyrell explains the function of the memory implants; and especially when he is confronted by a disillusioned and tearful Rachael.

What is happening is that the emotional distance, the lack of empathy required for Deckard to do his job, seems to be becoming harder for him to maintain – the opposite of what Philip K. Dick envisaged as the fate of warriors. Rather than becoming hardened to his task, Deckard finds himself empathising more and more with these artificial humans.

Deckard appears disturbed by this, as the process does not seem to be within his control. What then is causing these feelings? Is it his basic humanity continuing to assert itself or something else?

As his attachment to Rachael grows, not without a fight on his part, and especially after his encounter with the android philosopher, Roy Batty, Deckard renounces his role as Blade Runner and even his citizenship. He becomes an outlaw along with Rachael.

Is Deckard a replicant?

This is perhaps the question most asked about this film, especially with the deliberate inclusion of the unicorn sequence in *The Director's Cut.* Ridley Scott has stated in an interview that it certainly was his intention to have Deckard and the audience discover that the Blade Runner was a replicant at the end of the narrative.

There is a problem with this, though. Deckard lacks many of the attributes of the replicant – the strength, the ability to withstand extreme conditions (remember Leon's demonstration at Chew's place), the intelligence. Would Bryant send a weak, not-so-smart replicant out in pursuit of really strong and smart ones? Does part of the obtuseness of the film arise from the confusion of the director himself and the opportunity he had in *The Director's Cut* to have second thoughts about it? Or did Scott make the statement simply to stimulate argument?

Some students of the film believe Scott's statement spoils one of the most interesting questions raised by *Blade Runner*: the question of what it is that truly separates the human from even the most cleverly designed machine. If Deckard is a replicant, then of what value is his struggle with his conscience? Is what we see in this film a man weighing up the relative merit of his social conditioning against his innate humanity, or is the Deckard we see just a programmed machine exceeding its programming by developing emotions in a way unforeseen by its creators? Does the fact that Deckard is an android make his struggle any less engaging or valuable?

These are the questions that you certainly should address in your discussions about this character.

Roy Batty (Rutger Hauer)

Replicant (M) Des: Batty (Roy)
Nexus-6 N6MAA10816
Incept date: 8 Jan., 2016
Func: Combat, Colonization, Defence Program
Phys: Lev A *Mental: Lev. A*

Just as the director obviously enjoyed playing with viewers' expectations of the character of the 'hard-bitten cop', so he toys with any preconceptions about 'nasty, vicious, killer androids'.

Roy Batty is introduced as the leader of a band of mutinous replicants who have 'slaughtered twenty-three people' in their efforts to return to Earth, where they will wreak unforeseen havoc. As his statistics show, he was created for combat, with the highest mental and physical capabilities. He is the perfect killing machine. With his bleached crew-cut and chiselled features, we expect him to be a two-dimensional killer.

However, we are not allowed to rest on our first impressions. Roy shows tenderness and vulnerability in the scenes with Pris, and has obvious difficulty in handling the strength of his emotions when he comes face to face with his creator, Tyrell, and realises that his precious life must end. His capability for wonder and reflection, and especially his recognition of Deckard's desperation to cling to life, propel Roy far beyond this stereotype.

In the scene on the rooftop, our allegiance slowly moves away from Deckard, who becomes almost snivelling in his pathetic attempts to stay alive, to Roy, who emerges as a proud, philosophical, dignified and gracious being.

Scott deliberately blurs the expected definition of hero and villain, of human and replicant, so that the audience is forced to re-evaluate the characters and to participate in the narrative of the film rather than just watch it.

Rachael (Sean Young)

Rachael Tyrell is yet another character who undergoes a transformation in the course of the film. She begins as an aloof businesswoman: calm, controlled and in complete command of the situation. Her initial attitude towards Deckard is one of bored condescension. He is beneath her contempt in trying to find fault with the work of her uncle's corporation, with which she identifies completely.

When her world crumbles and she realises that she is a replicant and no more than an 'experiment', the result of a shrewd commercial decision, her tough facade disappears and she becomes an innocent, vulnerable and exploited being.

We cannot fail to sympathise with her plight. Everything on which she has ever depended for her identity and her security is revealed as no more substantial than the photograph she throws to the floor. What real choice does she have other than to depend on Deckard, the man who has been assigned to kill her? Her fate is always in someone else's hands.

Keep in mind that Rachael may indeed be a Nexus-7. She is alone (or is she?) in having memory implants, which lead her to believe that she is human. The other replicants know that they are not.

Pris (Daryl Hannah)

Replicant (F) Des: Pris
NEXUS-6 N6FAB21416
Incept date: 14 Feb., 2016
Func: Military/Leisure
Phys: Lev A *Mental: Lev. B*

Pris was created by Tyrell for the entertainment of military personnel stationed Off-world – a body to be exploited. Bryant calls her 'your basic pleasure model'. Cynically, her mental level has been designated as 'B' and her incept date is Valentine's Day.

On Earth, she shows signs of following her primary design function when she seduces J.F. with the promise of friendship and possibly physical contact (she wraps her legs around him – see Scene 20). Apart from this, however, Pris seems to be an innocent who loves Roy and relies on him to look after her. She fights for her life against Deckard and we feel pity for her even as we realise that her death throes are not human.

Zhora (Joanna Cassidy)

Replicant (F) Des: Zhora
NEXUS-6 N6FAB61216
Incept Date: 12 June, 2016
Func: Retrained (9 Feb., 2018) Polit. Homicide
Phys: Lev. A *Mental: Lev. B*

Zhora was designed in her retraining to be a political assassin. Bryant says of her, 'Talk about Beauty and the Beast – she's both' (Scene 5).

When we meet her, we are certainly struck by her beautiful body, but she, like Pris, is being exploited: this time as a stripper in a seedy club. Although she becomes suspicious of Deckard and tries to strangle him, our sympathies are then invoked as she flees, desperate and incredibly vulnerable in her see-through plastic outfit. She certainly doesn't look like a member of a 'kick murder squad' as she crashes through plate glass windows and onto the footpath.

Female versus male characters

There has been some discussion of the fact that Scott's female characters are two-dimensional and that the narrative interest centres far too much on the males, Deckard and Roy Batty.

We certainly don't gain much insight into the motivation or thoughts of Rachael, Pris or Zhora. Are they just convenient milestones in Deckard's psychological journey, or do they have a life of their own?

See 'Sexism' on pp.45–6 for further discussion of gender roles and power relations in *Blade Runner*.

Leon (Brion James)

Replicant (M) Des: Leon
NEXUS-6 N6 MAC 41717
Incept Date: 10 April, 2017
Func: Combat/Loader (Nuc. Fiss.)
Phys: Lev. A Mental: Lev. C

Leon is only a minor character, but he is representative of the cynical way in which Tyrell worked towards his goal of commerce. While Leon was a physically outstanding specimen, he was designed for combat and the extremely hazardous task of working with nuclear weapons. Because his function was a purely physical one, no circuits were wasted on his brain; his mental level was 'C'. We are meant to notice this in his V-K test, where he finds it difficult to concentrate and keeps going off at tangents. He is also the least able to handle his emerging emotional responses. This is probably why he loses control and shoots Holden, putting the lives of all the other replicants at risk.

Gaff (Edward James Olmos)

The ever-present, shadowy Gaff seems to hover over Deckard's every move. He is Mexican-Japanese and speaks a strange language, 'Cityspeak' – a mixture of Japanese, Spanish, German and guttertalk. He is small in stature and dresses very sharply in a suit, bow tie, hat and full-length coat. His eyes are a chilling pale blue.

Gaff seems to be very contemptuous of Deckard, leaving origami figures to comment on Deckard's cowardice (the chicken), his excitement at being involved in an investigation (the matchstick man) and finally his (possible) replicant status (the unicorn).

We are never told whether he is a Blade Runner or not, and his competitive attitude might suggest that he has not yet been elevated to that status. When, however, we realise that he has possibly had access to Deckard's memory implants and knows about the unicorn dream, we wonder whether he may not have been the real Blade Runner and Deckard just a convenient replicant tool.

We find we can't rely too much on this negative interpretation of Gaff when, in the final scene, we realise that he has allowed Rachael to live and has given Deckard a cryptic message that he will allow them both to escape. Even Gaff has empathy it seems.

Again, Ridley Scott has created a character who defies an easy judgement.

Tyrell (Joe Turkel)

Doctor Eldon Tyrell, although not drawn in a great amount of detail, is very significant in terms of the underlying themes of this text. He represents the scientific hierarchy of this disintegrating world. He puts commerce – power and monetary gain – ahead of relationships, love, loyalty and morality. He is completely Machiavellian in the way he uses his creations and other human beings in pursuit of his aims. 'Commerce is our goal here at Tyrell; more human than human is our motto', he says proudly (Scene 6).

When he is confronted by Roy, his arrogance and his lack of connection with real people is shown in his condescending treatment of his 'prodigal son'. He seems to have no comprehension of the anger that might be generated in someone who has been exploited and then discarded as Roy has been. His patronising reassurance, 'The light that burns twice as bright burns half as long' (Scene 22) only serves to further inflame Roy's righteous indignation.

While we are shocked and horrified at the cold-blooded and vicious way in which Roy ends Tyrell's life, we do not feel that he is any great loss to society.

J.F. Sebastian (William Sanderson)

Sebastian is a truly innocent man. Although he is a brilliant genetic engineer, he has not been able to leave Earth because of a condition that causes him to age prematurely, Methuselah Syndrome. He is pathologically lonely and seems without connection to any other human being (as, by the way, do all the other humans we meet). He uses his formidable skills to create his own friends, the Kaiser, Bear and others, which he programs to greet him enthusiastically when he arrives home. When we see this we are amused, but we are also struck by how emotionally impoverished his life is.

Sebastian presents a perfect target for Pris and Roy. He is delighted to have company and only fleetingly suspects their motives. Even when he becomes uncomfortable with their demands, he doesn't have the force of personality to withstand them. We are left wondering why Roy finds it necessary to kill someone so harmless.

A note on names

In literature, it is always worth examining the names of characters. Writers and directors enjoy playing with words. Sometimes the names they give to characters provide an insight into who the characters are. When discussing Gaff, for example, a check of the dictionary produces some interesting definitions: 'gaff, barbed fishing spear; stick with an iron hook for landing large fish' and 'blow the gaff, let out plot or secret', and 'gaffer...foreman of gang of workmen'. Where does the word Pris come from? The dictionary may also be useful in understanding who she is. On the other hand, Batty has an obvious connotation that doesn't help us to understand the character at all.

THEMES, IDEAS & VALUES

The themes of *Blade Runner* are particularly interesting because they relate not only to the text itself, but also to Ridley Scott's vision (or fears?) about where our world may be heading, and to the kinds of eternal questions that intrigue everyone and have engaged the greatest thinkers since the beginning of humankind.

You may notice that there is quite a deal of overlap between the various themes so that discussion of one invariably leads into another. This is a tribute to the complexity and wholeness of the director's vision and the skill with which the themes are woven into each other and into the story.

Humanity

We human beings take great pride in our superior status on this planet. We don't really like to see ourselves as merely the highest animal on the evolutionary ladder; rather we like to focus on the qualitative differences between *homo sapiens* and other 'sentient beings'. Similarly, we tend to be uncomfortable with the idea of machines becoming too 'clever', comforting ourselves with the thought that behind every computer is a living, breathing, 'human' person with his or her finger on the 'Off' button.

The possibility of human reproductive cloning continues to both fascinate and horrify us, and to trouble our sense of who we are. If human life can be created in a petri dish, then where is its sanctity, its mystery? Aren't we far more than a clump of created cells?

In *Blade Runner*, Ridley Scott explores these very questions. What if humans were to discover a way to replicate themselves? What if these creations evolved beyond their creators? How dangerous would this be?

So what is it that makes us human? Thousands of writers have addressed this issue, but you should think and write about it for yourself as well as asking others what they think.

In *Do Androids Dream of Electric Sheep?* Philip K. Dick focused on empathy, the capacity to feel for and with another being, so that the pain (or joy) is shared. It is quite different and much more complex than either sympathy or pity, which are more removed from the person experiencing the emotions. For Dick, it 'is empathy that in the end, is finally what distinguishes the human from the machine, the spiritual from the mechanical, authentic from even the most cunningly created pseudo-life.' Scott delves deeply into this idea in *Blade Runner*. As the film unfolds, you will see Deckard, who presumably starts out as a human who had to repress his natural empathy to become a cold-blooded killer, gradually lose his control over his feelings, while Roy, who starts out with no empathy, gradually develops it. Roy shows the development of his empathetic response when, in the climactic scene, he understands how much Deckard wants to live – and cannot kill him or let him die.

But empathy is not the only difference that has been argued as distinguishing humans from animals and machines. Consider the chart below. Can you think of some more categories? Gauge the characters in *Blade Runner* on some of these criteria. What category should they be in?

Human	**Animal**	**Machine**
Is able to plan	Operates only from instinct	Can plan only if programmed to do so
Is able to reason	Motivated only by survival	Reasons according to programming
Has moral principles, a conscience	Operates only on instinct	Has no moral principles
Has free will	Instinct, not free will, guides actions	Has no free will; cannot operate outside programming
Is able to love	Incapable of love; mates from instinct in order for species to survive	Incapable of love or other emotions; operates only according to logic

Can learn from mistakes	Learning limited to what will enable it to survive	Corrects mistakes only if programmed to do so
Feels fear, guilt, remorse, grief, loss	Feels none of this	Feels none of this
Is basically good	Good/evil is irrelevant	Good/evil is irrelevant
Emotional depth and control grows with maturity	No such growth occurs	No such growth occurs
Is capable of reflection	Is incapable of reflection	Is incapable of reflection
Questions the meaning of life, the universe and everything	Does not question the meaning of life	Doesn't question anything unless programmed to do so
Is naturally curious	Can be curious	Is curious only if programmed to be
Feels pity, sympathy, empathy for others	Feels none of this	Feels none of this
Seeks out and enjoys relationships with others; tends to live in families and communities	Some animals seek out the company of others or live in families	Has no need for company or family

After reading the chart, you may be feeling quite smugly superior, but there is another, darker side to humanity. Humankind may have many capabilities not possessed by either animals or machines, but this development also has its costs. With free will comes the choice to do evil, and, although most humans have moral principles and a conscience, it is certainly possible to override them. More frightening still, there are those humans who seem to have missed out on the development of any conscience at all. They are not guided by the desire to do the right thing but rather by self-advancement, greed, lust or power. In their very extreme form, these people are known as psychopaths or sociopaths.

Further on the down side, in being human we also inherit human frailty – the ability to make mistakes, to have accidents, to make wrong choices and decisions. We can also hurt others and ourselves, both literally and figuratively.

So you can see that 'the human condition' is a very complex and varied state of being. It seems that we are certainly capable of more than either animals or machines, but this 'more' is not necessarily always for the good.

In the film, Ridley Scott delves deeply into the theme of humanity. Nexus-6 replicants are consciously designed to be like humans in every way except their emotions. This makes them incredibly effective combatants as they are incapable of feeling either fear or empathy for their opponents. Their incapacity for reflection also makes them obedient slaves. However, as Tyrell tells Deckard, after a time they do begin to develop emotional responses of their own. It seems to us that they are developing far more than just emotions; they are becoming reflective and searching beings. That is why they are attempting to return to Earth – to find their Creator, to ask the questions that we all want answered: 'Who am I? What does life mean? How long do I have?' In a sense, they are becoming human.

On the other hand, when we meet Deckard we see a human who spends his life on the knife's edge between humanity and artificial life, first identifying and then destroying rebellious replicants. As a result of his occupation, he has been forced to eliminate emotion and empathy from his life. He cannot afford to feel anything for the beings he 'retires', so he must objectify them. To kill them he has had to become like them.

This scenario, although extreme, is not entirely unfamiliar. We have all heard of doctors, ambulance men or police officers who, in order to protect their emotions and to do their jobs effectively, become hardened to the plight of the people with whom they deal each day, even to the point of seeming callous or uncaring. It is not that they are inhuman; what we see in their professional lives is a defence mechanism against the trauma of their daily experiences. In their personal lives, most are probably as emotional and loving as anyone else. Some, though, do not fare so well; the defence takes over their minds and their lives, sometimes with unfortunate consequences.

In *Blade Runner,* we see an interesting twist. Although experienced in his role as a Blade Runner, Deckard cannot maintain this emotional detachment. His humanity continually reasserts itself and he ultimately finds himself empathising with his victims to the point where he can no longer continue in his job. The other part of the twist is that, at the same time as we see Deckard wrestling with his conscience, we can clearly see that the replicants are becoming far more like humans than they are like machines.

As the film proceeds, the line between human and replicant becomes more and more blurred, culminating in Roy's saving of his hunter's life. Watching Deckard's desperate fight, he empathises with him to such an extent that his instinct is to reach out. Looking at Roy Batty's face at this point, it seems he is as amazed as we are by the strength of his feelings.

In playing with the distinction between human and non-human, Ridley Scott takes away our security blanket and forces us to re-define humanity. We find it very difficult to identify with Tyrell, a human who uses everyone else for his stated aim, 'commerce'. Instead we find ourselves identifying more and more with the replicants, who, although they do 'some questionable things', show more humanity than most of the 'real' humans.

Many fans of the movie reject Scott's suggestion that Deckard is a replicant as they believe that this would make a mockery of everything he learns throughout the course of the film. They see a machine developing past its programming as less worthy than a man re-defining his moral stance in the world. They may be right, but perhaps Scott's point is that it doesn't matter whether a character is human or a replicant; it is possible for us to become equally engaged by their search for meaning.

Ask yourself, who is the 'most human' character in the film, and who the least?

Identity: memories, photographs and the past

Our identity is that collection of qualities, characteristics and experiences that makes us the unique individuals we are. If you answer the questions, 'Who are you? What are you like?' you will come pretty close to summing up your identity. Although this sounds simple, these questions can be very difficult for us to answer. Human beings are constantly reviewing and changing their ideas about who they are throughout their lives.

A significant theme in *Blade Runner* is the reliance that human beings place on memories and photographs as a guide to identity and the solidity of the past. When Deckard discovers that Rachael is a replicant, Tyrell proudly boasts that he has developed the use of memory implants as a method of controlling his latest Nexus-6 replicants (see notes on Scene 6). In order to make her easier to control, Rachael has been provided with a whole range of childhood memories that she believes to be real; she also has a set of photographs, which for her 'prove' that the past is a reality and that she is who she believes herself to be.

When Deckard cruelly explodes her illusions, telling her about the baby spiders and playing doctor with her brother (Scene 12), she instantly loses all the foundations on which she has built her identity. Her whole personal history was tied up in these flimsy things – she trusted them implicitly, but now she knows them to be worthless. She is left with nothing to trust – no family, no past, nothing on which to base her identity.

Deckard is strangely disturbed by Tyrell's revelations of his manipulative use of memory and by the ensuing confrontation with Rachael. After she leaves, he reviews his own past, arraying his 'proof' on his piano, also a concrete symbol of earlier times. As he ponders, the director gives us a glimpse into Deckard's own memory: a pure white unicorn galloping free through a forest. As viewers we understand why Deckard is disturbed, but then we are shocked to realise that one of the very memories with which he comforts himself is itself a fabrication. In this respect Deckard is the same as Rachael, constructing identity from fabricated memories. Note that the replicants' memories are all tagged to actual objects, concrete events in the past and people shown in photographs. They are of the 'real' world. Deckard, though, remembers a fantasy. Perhaps one distinction between humans and non-humans is the ability to fantasise. But then, Roy takes a very abstract and detached view in the last few minutes of his life, and that is fantasy. Empathy might also be described as fantasy.

In having his characters question the role of memories and photographs, Ridley Scott is prompting us to do the same. As we see how much Deckard and Rachael rely on these ephemeral things, we become as concerned as they do. If we can't rely on memories and photographs to tell us who we are and what our past was, then what is our anchor?

As the film goes on, we become more and more aware that it is only through relationships with others that we can know the truth of our identity and our past. We learn who we are through and with others. The replicants know who they are because of their shared past, their love for and loyalty to each other. At the end of the film, Rachael and Deckard speak of 'love' and 'trust' as their new anchors. Strangely, all of the other characters in the film seem almost totally isolated. What then do they have to rely on for their identity?

Alienation versus relationships

If you say that someone is alienated, you are suggesting that they are emotionally or intellectually separated from others or from their society as a whole.

Just as it is easier to know who you are when you have a shared past, so a healthy community needs to be built on relationships: families, religious groups, schools, sporting groups – any group that brings people together through shared interests. A network of positive relationships provides us with a strong sense of self, physical and emotional security and a structure for approaching the world.

Most sociologists would say that our society is becoming more and more fragmented. Divorce rates are on the rise, membership of churches has collapsed, mental and health care is becoming harder to access, cities are growing in size while a sense of community is becoming harder and harder to maintain. Alienation, one of the results of this fragmentation, is seen as a leading contributor to mental illness, homelessness, drug addiction and crime.

Ridley Scott was evidently aware of this trend in our world today, as he depicts almost all of his human characters as living in total isolation from each other. In *Blade Runner* we see the leaders of society conducting their lives in physical, intellectual and emotional isolation from the ordinary citizens – and each other. Tyrell and Sebastian play chess by phone. Chew and Sebastian live and work alone. Bryant, Gaff and Deckard are linked only by their work (although Gaff finally appears to show some empathy for Deckard). Look at the 'human background' of the film: even the 'little people' are shown as being an aggregation of separate individuals, not groups. The main character, Deckard, is so alienated that the only beings he interacts with are the replicants he is paid to hunt down and kill.

In developing notes on this theme, look at the following elements.

The characters' physical surroundings:

- Sebastian in his deserted building
- Deckard perched in his ninety-seventh floor eyrie like a lone eagle
- Chew in his Ice House
- Tyrell in his fortress.

Emotional distances between characters:

- Tyrell's attitude to Rachael and Roy
- Bryant's attitude to the replicants
- Deckard's attitude towards his prey.

Intellectual or philosophical differences between characters:

- Tyrell's conversation with Roy
- Roy's speech on the rooftop.

As you look at the text in this way, you might notice that the replicants are not alienated from each other; neither can Deckard maintain his emotional distance from Rachael for long. Perhaps Scott is suggesting that alienation is not a normal state of affairs and that beings, whether human or not, are drawn to each other and towards relationship rather than alienation?

Scott gives us a further clue as to his thoughts on this matter in the way he directs our sympathies towards his characters. We feel very little for the heartless Tyrell, even as Roy brutally kills him. We are repulsed by the way the slimy Inspector Bryant threatens Deckard so that he will return to duty, an action that immediately blurs the boundary between the employment of a human with 'free will' and a slave replicant. We certainly feel far more for the vulnerable Pris and Zhora, for Leon and his 'precious photos' and for Roy as he grieves for Pris. Scott evidently intends that we favour those characters who seek out and value their associations with others.

Class distinction

Class distinction also has to do with the relationships and with many of the values underlying the structure of the society in which *Blade Runner* is set. The threat that carries the greatest weight with Deckard is that, if he doesn't return to duty as a Blade Runner, he will become one of the 'little people' (Scene 4). Bryant implies that his privileges will be revoked and that he will have to fight for survival with the teeming masses of Los Angeles. The speed with which Deckard acquiesces tells us a great deal about just how difficult it might be to live without the protection of the Police Department and the Tyrell Corporation.

You should divide the characters of *Blade Runner* into 'little people' and the 'elite'. What is it that gives people status in 2019? Has the growth of technology created a 'technological elite', a futuristic aristocracy who, through their monopoly of science and technology rather than, say, the ownership of land, have more status, power and money than the rest? What evidence is there that Scott believes this to be a good thing? Does he direct our sympathies towards the elite or the 'rest'? Who do we want to 'win' in the end? Who does win, if anyone?

You might also draw parallels with the present. What are the things that divide our present society? Are control of information and technology very important? Historically, what has divided societies?

Technology and scientific development

In *Blade Runner,* Ridley Scott investigates some of the 'What if ...?' questions of science fiction. What would our world be like if technology were to develop to the stage where technocrats like Bill Gates became rulers of the world? What if technology could create a being that took on an emotional life of its own, perhaps even becoming 'more human' than its creator? The answers to these questions are provided in the storyline of this movie – and they are disturbing answers.

As science fiction has always done, this film raises particular questions confronting contemporary society. It invites us to examine them in another era, another setting (even another universe in many sci-fi works) so we can look at them in the abstract without being blinded by current knowledge and the real world. What warning might Scott be giving his viewers about the development of science and technology? What ethical questions arise in *Blade Runner* about the value of life? You might like to connect this theme with such matters as cloning, frozen embryo disposal or embryo research. What is more important – survival, the development of technology or respect for human life? Who should be responsible for the control of such developments?

Care of the environment

Ridley Scott examines the three interrelated issues of environmental care, global warming and over-population by setting his story in a world that has been devastated by neglect – devastated to such an extent that the population is being moved, quite urgently it seems, to other planets 'Off-world'. Over-population and the relentless, selfish exploitation of the environment has led to Earth's rejection of her human parasites. The ever-present blimps, with their constant barrage of information about the delights of Off-world, suggest that it will not be long before Earth becomes uninhabitable.

This message impresses less in Australia than it would in the United States and Europe, where areas of gross pollution exist and the consequences are becoming very obvious. Old-time Los Angeles residents talk about a time when they were able to see the Sierra reaching high into the sky on their western horizon; today's L.A. residents talk about how wonderful it would be to be able to see to the edge of the city. As city pollution increases, those who can afford it move further out – off-city as it were. In Europe, entire forests are being stripped by acid rain. Many forests are simply regrowth; in Germany, no tree exists older than about eighty to ninety years.

Although perhaps a minor theme, it interrelates with many of the others to paint a picture of a crumbling natural world that is winding down into oblivion. You should look at how this theme might be connected to those of alienation, empathy or relationships.

Sexism

Sexism is the belief that the members of one sex, usually women, are less intelligent or less capable than those of the other sex and need not be treated equally.

It was suggested earlier that you should examine the female characters presented in this text. It seems at first glance that in the world of 2019 sexism abounds. Female characters are 'basic pleasure models' (Pris), 'Beauty and the Beast' (Zhora) or 'an experiment, nothing more' (Rachael).

But is this sexism or replicantism (to coin a word)? We see both Pris and Zhora fight for their lives as ferociously as any male character (they lose out, but so does Leon). The Cambodian woman who examines the scale with her electron microscope is clearly highly educated and an expert who is trusted in that role. When Tyrell introduces Rachael, it is as a senior executive in the Tyrell corporation.

But it is the male characters who hold the major roles and the power in *Blade Runner*. This might be because Scott wanted to avoid issues like sexism and sexual attraction (apart from the mandatory love interest) diverting attention away from the central big issue he is tackling – what it is to be a human being.

Is sexism demonstrated? It is an issue worth looking at; the exploitation and abuse of Pris, Rachael and Zhora point us in that direction. But then the male characters are also threatened, abused and treated with contempt.

Bureaucracy and the Big Brother syndrome

Control and loss of privacy have been preoccupations for sci-fi writers and film-makers since the beginning of the genre. Long before 'real' computers came into existence, they began warning against the potential of technology to bring together vast masses of data resulting in the loss of privacy and an excessive control over individuals.

In George Orwell's *Nineteen Eighty-Four*, Big Brother was the enigmatic head of state that citizens only ever saw as a disembodied face on huge posters that loomed over the city streets. The Thought Police were agents of Big Brother; they had telescreens and microphones in every household through which they monitored the citizens' every action. Anything out of the ordinary could lead to an accusation of 'thought crime'.

While Scott's Los Angeles has not developed the Big Brother scenario to this extent, the blimps and police in flying Spinners do seem to follow every move. Gaff apparently has no trouble picking up Deckard at the noodle bar. The police are not evident as Deckard pursues Zhora but they are right on the spot when he kills her. As Deckard enters the Bradbury Building, the hovering police demand identification and an explanation of his activity. Gaff pops into view at the decisive moment after Roy dies, and he has already visited Deckard's apartment. This, along with the oppressive climactic conditions and crowded streetscape, create a world where there is little privacy or personal space. The police (bureaucracy) and the Tyrell Corporation (technocracy) seem to have control over almost every detail of the lives of the citizens.

It is Scott's intention that the audience should be made to feel a little uncomfortable while watching this film. You should feel the dampness of the insistent rain dripping down your collar; you should feel hemmed-in and intimidated by the jostling people, the looming, droning blimps, the lurking Spinners. Would you like to live in such a world?

Before we feel too complacent, perhaps we should look around for 'Big Brother' tendencies in our own society. How are you limited and controlled in the decisions you make about your life? How are bureaucracies, multinational companies and technocrats dominating our society? Perhaps Scott's portrayal of a future society also carries a warning.

Eyes – a recurring motif

Ridley Scott makes a point of developing the motif of eyes throughout the movie. Some examples are:

- the huge, staring eye in the opening scene
- the Voigt-Kampff test, which uses pupil dilation to gauge emotional responses
- the luminous, unnaturally glowing quality of the replicants' eyes (note that Scott sometimes gives us a hint of this in Deckard's eyes as a clue to his possible replicant nature)
- Chew, the eye-maker, who can tell Roy and Leon are Nexus-6 'by your eyes'
- Leon's intended method of killing Deckard
- Roy's method of murdering Tyrell.

In highlighting eyes, Scott is on strong literary ground. Poets and novelists throughout the ages have referred to the eyes as 'the windows of the soul' and the purveyor of feelings, particularly the deepest human feelings that cannot be adequately conveyed by words.

The focus on eyes also has a strong basis in folk experience. People say that a person's eyes tell you more than anything else about the way they are feeling. If you watch someone smile or cry, grimace in pain, show surprise or sympathy, then you will see that the eyes play a major part in expressing the full range of human emotions. We acknowledge this in everyday life when we say someone who was faking pleasure at meeting us 'was not smiling with their eyes'. When we talk to someone, we look into their eyes and expect them to look at ours. If someone fails to look directly at us, we might assume that they are lying or concealing something . Somehow we feel that when we look into another person's eyes, we are connecting with the essence of their being.

Scott (and the author of the original novel) designed the V-K test to record pupil dilation in response to emotional stimuli in order to distinguish between humans and replicants. Like all good science fiction, it has some grounding in science. Iris movement in response to emotional stimuli is scientifically proven and is routinely measured in psychological laboratories. The movement of the iris, enlarging or shrinking the pupil, is one of the many cues we pick up, more or less unconsciously, when we are interacting with others. (We tend to think someone is friendly if their pupils enlarge when they see us.) Psychology has also shown that psychopaths have different emotional responses to normal people, failing to respond in the 'proper human' way to terms like 'mother'.

In the replicants' case, it is impossible to look beyond their eyes; their eyes are blank, opaque and seem to reflect rather than absorb light. Their eyes are not windows on any soul. When tested on emotional stimuli using the V-K test, they fail to respond. They don't give anything away or betray any emotion, because there is nothing to give away. They have no soul and no emotions. They are not human.

But how good a test is this? How does the outcome of Leon's test fit with a picture of an emotionless automaton? Was he upset? Emotional? What about other behaviour displayed by the replicants? Were there routine signs of emotion, introspection, love and loyalty?

COMPARISON OF DIFFERENT VERSIONS

There have been many versions of this film, including working prints and several 'sneak preview' cuts that were used to gauge viewer response. The most obvious comparison, however, is between the first cinema release (1982) and *The Director's Cut* (1992).

The Director's Cut versus the first cinema release

The significant differences between these two film versions are the use of a voice-over in the first cinema release and the hopeful sunset at its conclusion; and the inclusion of the unicorn dream in *The Director's Cut*.

Voice-over

There is no Philip Marlowe-style narration in *The Director's Cut*. (The character of Philip Marlowe featured in Raymond Chandler's hardboiled detective novels, several of which became classic film noirs, such as *The Big Sleep*.) The weary voice-over was part of Scott's original vision of the film as following in the tradition of film noir. Another reason for its original inclusion was in response to audience criticism in previews that the storyline was too hard to follow.

Scott deleted the voice-over in *The Director's Cut* partly because he believed that it was too grating and intrusive, and partly because he wanted the film to remain mysterious and open to interpretation. He wanted to ask questions, not necessarily answer them. As one of the crew said, 'a lot of things we did on *Blade Runner* were "possibly it's this or possibly it's that".'

The hopeful sunset

The last scene in the 1982 version of *Blade Runner* has Deckard and Rachael driving off in Deckard's sedan. Accompanied by uplifting music and a hopeful narration, they are seen driving through a verdant landscape with a beautiful blue sky above them.

A happy ending had always been considered, but it did not become definite until after the 'sneak previews'. This scene was the last to be shot in post-production and was included in response to poor audience reaction to the ambiguous lift scene. The 'wilderness footage' was actually borrowed from out-takes from Stanley Kubrick's *The Shining*.

In *The Director's Cut*, Scott returned to the ambiguous ending, which he believed was truer to the overall setting and mood of the film and left more to the viewer's imagination.

The unicorn dream

When Deckard is sitting at his piano, musing about his past (Scene 13), he has a vivid dream of a unicorn galloping through a lush green forest. This scene was not included in the first release as some of the producers considered it to be too vague. Scott, however, had always been very keen to include it because it strengthened his vision of Deckard as a replicant. How could an authentic human have a 'memory' of something that has never existed? It also ties in with Gaff's origami unicorn, which Deckard discovers in the final scene. This was one of the scenes filmed and added during post-production in England.

The legend of the unicorn had long fascinated Ridley Scott; in fact he explored it again in his next film, *Legend*. There is only ever one unicorn at any one time; as the old one dies a new one is born. The unicorn is only able to express love and happiness and can be tamed only by a virginal young woman. Is there anyone who fits any of these descriptions in *Blade Runner*?

Film versus novel

Philip K. Dick was a well known and prolific writer of science fiction short stories and novels. In 1968 he published a novel, *Do Androids Dream of Electric Sheep?*, in which he painted a picture of a post-holocaust dystopia where robots had evolved to such a stage that they were nearly indistinguishable from humans. Animals were so rare and precious after

'World War Terminus' that a real animal was the ultimate status symbol. Rick Deckard appeared in *Do Androids Dream of Electric Sheep?*; however, he was a hired bounty hunter rather than an elite policeman, and he took on the job of retiring the androids in order to make enough money to buy a real animal.

Rachael also appeared in the novel, but the idea of the androids developing emotions was not part of Dick's vision. As mentioned earlier, his preoccupation was with what separated man from machine. In his novel he investigated what might happen to a man whose job it was to kill other beings; what effect that might have on the empathy that Dick believed was the essential distinguishing feature of humans. The impetus for this novel was the Vietnam War. Dick was concerned about the morality of the war and the brutalisation of American soldiers in such a killing field.

So, while many of the details of the original story have been changed, the film stays true to the moral, philosophical and sociological issues it addressed. Philip K. Dick was quite involved, not always happily, in the making of the film, and died in the year of its first release.

QUESTIONS & ANSWERS

This section of the text guide focuses on your own analytical writing on *Blade Runner*, and gives you strategies for producing high-quality responses in your coursework and essays.

Essay writing – an overview

An essay on a literary work is a formal and serious piece of writing that presents your point of view on the text, usually in response to a given topic. Your 'point of view' in an essay is your interpretation of the meaning of the text's language, structure, characters, situations and events, supported by detailed analysis of textual evidence.

Analyse – don't summarise

In your essays it is important to avoid simply summarising what happens in a text.

- A **summary** is a description or paraphrase (retelling in different words) of the characters and events. For example: 'Macbeth has a horrifying vision of a dagger dripping with blood before he goes to murder King Duncan.'
- An **analysis** is an explanation of the real meaning or significance that lies 'beneath' the text's words (and images, for a film). For example: 'Macbeth's vision of a bloody dagger shows how deeply uneasy he is about the violent act he is contemplating – as well as his sense that supernatural forces are impelling him to act.'

A limited amount of summary is sometimes necessary to let your reader know which part of the text you wish to discuss. However, always keep this to a minimum and follow it immediately with your analysis of what this part of the text is really telling us.

Plan your essay

Carefully plan your essay so that you have a clear idea of what you are going to say. The plan ensures that your ideas flow logically, that your argument remains consistent and that you stay on the topic. An essay plan should be a list of **brief dot points** – no more than half a page.

- Include your central argument or main contention – a concise statement (usually in a single sentence) of your overall response to the topic. See 'Analysing an essay topic' for guidelines on how to formulate a main contention.
- Write three or four dot points for each paragraph indicating the main idea and evidence/examples from the text. Note that in your essay you will need to *expand* on these points and *analyse* the evidence.

Structure your essay

An essay is a complete, self-contained piece of writing. It has a clear beginning (the introduction), middle (several body paragraphs) and end (the last paragraph or conclusion). It must also have a central argument that runs throughout, linking each paragraph to form a coherent whole.

See an example of an introduction and a conclusion in the 'Sample answer' section.

The introduction establishes your overall response to the topic. It includes your main contention and outlines the main evidence you will refer to in the course of the essay. Write your introduction *after* you have done a plan and *before* you write the rest of the essay.

The body paragraphs argue your case – they present evidence from the text and explain how this evidence supports your argument. Each body paragraph needs:

- **a strong topic sentence** (usually the first sentence) that states the main point being made in the paragraph
- **evidence** from the text, including some brief quotations
- **analysis** of the textual evidence explaining its significance and **explanation** of how it supports your argument
- **links back to the topic** in one or more statements, usually towards the end of the paragraph.

Connect the body paragraphs so that your discussion flows smoothly. Use some linking words and phrases like 'similarly' and 'on the other hand', though don't start every paragraph like this. Another strategy is to use a significant word from the last sentence of one paragraph in the first sentence of the next.

Use key terms from the topic – or similes for them – throughout, so the relevance of your discussion to the topic is always clear.

The conclusion ties everything together and finishes the essay. It includes strong statements that emphasise your central argument and provide a clear response to the topic.

Avoid simply restating the points made earlier in the essay – this will end on a very flat note and imply that you have run out of ideas and vocabulary. The conclusion is meant to be a logical extension of what you have written, not just a repetition or summary. Writing an effective conclusion can be a challenge. Try using these tips:

- Start by linking back to the final sentence of the second-last paragraph – this helps your writing to 'flow', rather than leaping back to your main contention straight away.
- Use similes and expressions with equivalent meanings to vary your vocabulary. This allows you to reinforce your line of argument without being repetitive.
- When planning your essay, think of one or two broad statements or observations about the text's wider meaning. These should be related to the topic and your overall argument. Keep them for the conclusion, since they will give you something 'new' to say but still follow logically from your discussion. The introduction will be focused on the topic, but the conclusion can present a wider view of the text.

Essay topics

1. The Tyrell Corporation has as its motto, 'More human than human'. Has it achieved its aim?
2. 'Technology has no answer for life's enduring problems: love, death and the meaning of life.' Discuss.

3 'In Ridley Scott's bleak vision of the future, Deckard has no more autonomy or control over his own life than do the replicants.' Do you agree?

4 'Memories and photographs are unreliable; relationships are the only true witnesses to the past.' Discuss.

5 'Any civilisation based on slavery is doomed.' Discuss.

6 'Humanity's fatal error is to fail to conceive that our creations may grow beyond us.' Is this idea supported in this film?

7 Does Deckard represent all that is left of humanity, or the next phase of pseudo-life?

8 If only the fearful, fragile and foolish are left on Earth, then why is Deckard still there?

9 '*Blade Runner* shows us a world in which the faults and shortcomings of our society are magnified.' Do you agree?

10 One reviewer wrote that the 'storyline is sometimes muddled and the film lacks dramatic momentum.' Do you agree?

11 'The members of the audience of the film *Blade Runner* have the same problem as the Blade Runner himself. We find it hard to tell just who is a replicant and who is not.' Discuss.

12 'Our sympathies in *Blade Runner* lie firmly with the replicants.' Do you agree?

13 'There is little hope or humanity in Ridley Scott's vision of our future.' Do you agree?

14 '*Blade Runner* provides a dismal view of the role of women in our society's future.' Discuss.

15 'Ridley Scott plays with our expectations of both the science fiction and film noir genres in his film *Blade Runner*.' Do you agree?

16 '*Blade Runner* presents humans as being merely concerned with power, money and possessions.' Do you agree?

17 'Humans and replicants are more alike than they are different.' Discuss.

18 "Too bad she won't live. But then again, who does?" 'Gaff's parting message to Deckard sums up one of the major messages of the film.' Do you agree?

19 'There are no heroes in this film'. Discuss.

20 'Batty is the only character in this film who displays real human qualities.' Do you agree?

21 'The hero of *Blade Runner* turns out to be Roy Batty rather than Deckard.' Do you agree?

22 '*Blade Runner* is an uneasy but compelling glimpse of what life in the twenty-first century may hold for human-kind.' Discuss.

23 'Scott's extraordinary production design is aesthetically pleasing but it adds nothing to the meaning of the film.' Do you agree?

24 'Scott makes a big mistake in insisting that Deckard is a replicant; this reduces the impact of his film.' Do you agree?

Analysing an essay topic: a seven-step approach

Be prepared to explore the issues presented in the text in a fluent and organised manner. It is very important that you plan your response. Here is a seven-step approach to the task.

1 Write the question in the centre of your page.

2 Circle or highlight the key terms, paying attention to any linking or qualifying words such as 'but' or 'most'.

3 Using arrows, write in a selection of working definitions/synonyms for the key terms. You should use a dictionary here if you are in any doubt as to the accurate definition.

4 Tease out the key questions/issues the topic is asking you to address. This is a crucial step in working out exactly what the question is asking (helpful if your task is to answer it!).

5 Begin to develop a line of argument in which you systematically work through these issues. You might like to jot down a few *brief* points here, then number them in the order you will present them

in the essay. Keep in mind that your discussion should be firmly tied to the text with the use of detailed references to scenes and brief quotations.

6 Write your introduction only when you have a clear idea of your complete line of argument. There is nothing worse than getting halfway through an essay only to find you have boxed yourself into a corner or changed your mind about what you want to say.

7 Write up your essay, remembering to finish with a paragraph that provides a logical conclusion to your argument.

Try not to simply accept or reject the quotation or question as it is presented. Attempt to qualify your answer or to show that you can see both sides of an issue.

Analysing a sample topic

Your planning procedure, following the steps outlined above, is as follows.

Steps 1&2: write out the question; underline key terms

'There is <u>little hope</u> or <u>humanity</u> left in <u>Ridley Scott's vision</u> of our <u>future</u>.' Do you <u>agree</u>?

Step 3: definitions

Dictionaries are useful for providing synonyms or helpful phrases for you to use in your essay. Synonyms for the key terms will show that you are on track without constantly repeating the same word:

- 'little' – only a very small amount, not much, present only to a small extent
- 'hope' – a feeling of desire or expectation that things will go well in the future, optimism
- 'humanity' (the integral term in the question) – the state of being a human being, rather than an animal or object; the quality of being kind, thoughtful and sympathetic towards others
- 'Ridley Scott's vision' – the director's view/idea
- 'agree' – have the same opinion.

Step 4: tease out key questions

Why are these the key terms? What is the question really asking?

This is perhaps the hardest step to deal with, so I'll go into a bit of detail here.

- 'Hope' and 'humanity' are obviously the key themes that this question is asking you to address. Each concept will need to be treated separately. If you mention only one of them, then you are missing half the question.
- 'Little' is one of those sneaky qualifying words that suggests there may still be *some* hope and/or humanity. It requires you to answer the question of exactly how much of these two qualities you see in Scott's world – none, a glimpse, or a great deal?
- 'Or' is another important word as it suggests that neither of these things is present to any significant extent in 2019. You may decide that there is one and not the other, or that both are present, but to answer the question fully you must recognise that this is what you are being asked to do.
- 'Ridley Scott's vision' indicates that you are required to discuss not just the characters and themes in the text, but also the director's intention – the message he was sending to the viewer about what he saw as a possible future for our world. How does Scott see the future of our world? How do we know that it is his intention that we see it this way?
- 'Agree' asks you to assess how far you go along with this statement. Many essay questions ask this. The readers want to know whether you agree entirely, in part, or not at all with the statement. Show evidence that you are able to weigh the truth of the statement against your knowledge of the text.

Step 5: line of argument

You would probably complete this in point form, but I'll just describe how you might develop a logical approach to this question.

For this essay you would begin by describing how hopeless and inhumane the world of *Blade Runner* seems to be. You would specifically mention Tyrell's commercially driven cruelty, the replicants' desperation, the alienation that seems to dominate the lives of all the humans we meet. You would mention the state of the Earth's environment, finally giving up as a result of man's exploitation and neglect and how man is in the process of deserting Earth for Off-world colonies. You would also refer to the consistency and detail with which the director presents this view to us, indicating that it is *his* vision. What hope can you see that any of this will change? Very little perhaps.

Note: a word that would be very useful here is 'dystopia' – the opposite of 'utopia', which is an imaginary perfect society in which everyone is happy. In a dystopia, society is dysfunctional and individuals are alienated and miserable.

You should then go on to assess whether the director's vision is entirely pessimistic. Are there any signs that you can see that humanity – kindness, thoughtfulness and sympathy for others – is alive and well in Scott's dystopian world? You might look here at J.F.'s innocence and trust, the loyalty and love obvious in the relationships among the replicants, Deckard's rejection of the values of the technocrats and his decision to risk everything with Rachael. You should also examine Roy's motives in saving Deckard's life on the rooftop, mentioning the ironic fact that humanity may be most evident in a being that is not 'human'. Does this mean that humanity is seen by Ridley Scott as such a strong force that it can grow and thrive even in artificial life? If so, is his view optimistic or pessimistic (the power of humanity versus humans as machines)?

Your conclusion should be the logical end point of your discussion, rather than a weak re-hash of your introduction. In this essay you should focus on your overall viewpoint about the message Scott's film was intended to convey about the future of humanity.

Step 6: the introduction

Now that you know where you are going, it should be easy to write your introduction. Your first paragraph should make it clear that you understand what it is that you are being required to assess. It should also provide some indication of the way you intend to approach the topic, without giving away your conclusion. Remember, the idea is to work your way through to your conclusion.

Step 7: write!

Try writing this response. It covers some of the essential themes of the text and it should help that you now have some structuring set out for you to build on.

SAMPLE ANSWER

'Given our sympathy for the replicants, it is science and technology which emerge as the real villains in *Blade Runner*.' Discuss.

The *Blade Runner* world of 2019 as created by Ridley Scott presents us with the breakdown of society: a dark gloomy world where science and technology have taken over. The city of Los Angeles is in a state of dystopia, where power and commercial success rule over compassion and empathy for human kind. Doctor Eldon Tyrell, director of the gargantuan Tyrell Corporation, has created a race of androids called replicants who were designed to be slaves but who have rebelled and returned to Earth in an attempt to extend their four-year life span. While the replicants are seen as the villains in this society, the viewer cannot help but sympathise with them and view science and technology, and those who control them, as the real villains.

The replicants were designed by Tyrell to be 'more human than human' in the sense that they would have superior strength and intelligence to humans. What the viewer witnesses, though, are replicants who are also in many ways more human, in terms of feeling emotions and empathy for others, than many of the 'real' humans in the film. The replicants do, however, also display the other side of humanity, which is the ability to do wrong and to make mistakes. But it is only as a result of technology that the replicants are forced to do 'questionable things' as they search for the answer to the question that all humans ask, 'How long do I have to live?' The replicants do show that they are capable of evil, but as the viewer understands that this is in an attempt to prolong their beloved and cherished lives, we cannot help but feel sympathy for them.

Given the viewers' feelings towards the replicants, it is science and technology, and in particular Tyrell, who holds the real power in this field, that the viewer considers the true villains. Tyrell shows no empathy or feeling towards either humanity or the replicants, thinking only of his God-like ambitions. His cruelty and lack of compassion are obvious when he refers to Rachael as 'an experiment, nothing more' and when he so condescendingly dismisses Roy Batty who comes to plead for 'more life'. The viewer feels no sympathy for Tyrell at any point in the film and it appears entirely just that in the end the maker is killed by his creation.

In the world of *Blade Runner*, the breakdown of communication and any sense of community are seen to be as a result of the ever-increasing prominence of science and technology. Giant billboards dominate the city and garish neon lights provide the only source of light. The city is crowded; the harsh noises and the Spinners flying above add to the confusion. This is a world where science and technology must be blamed for the overwhelming sense of claustrophobia and destruction and can be seen as the source of many of this society's problems.

It is hard to feel anything but sympathy for the replicants throughout the majority of *Blade Runner*. Although they sometimes act in a way that might be considered cruel and inhumane, the viewer must remember that this is how they were created to behave. They are simply fulfilling their design: a design created by the science that is the source of their world's problems. The fact that the replicants can develop past this design and the technology that created them is what is truly remarkable and raises the viewer's admiration.

REFERENCES & READING

The film

Blade Runner: The Director's Cut 1992, Time Warner. Directed by Ridley Scott.

Books

Dick, Philip K. 1968, *Do Androids Dream of Electric Sheep?*, Harper Collins, London.

Kerman, Judith B. (ed.) 1991, *Retrofitting Blade Runner: Issues in Ridley Scott's Blade Runner and Philip K. Dick's Do Androids Dream of Electric Sheep*, Bowling Green State University Popular Press, Bowling Green Ohio.

Sammon, Paul 1996, *Future Noir: The Making of Blade Runner*, Orion Media, London.

Websites

BRMOVIE.COM, http://brmovie.com/
Contains extensive information about the film, including character, cast and crew profiles, details about sets and locations, essays on the film's themes and a *Blade Runner* encyclopaedia; also has downloadable versions of both the original and Director's Cut scripts.

BladeZone, http://www.bladezone.com/
Includes exclusive interviews with cast and crew and an archive of articles, essays and reports.

Blade Runner Insight, http://br-insight.com/
Presents articles and archives dating back to 1995.

The Official Blade Runner On-line Magazine, http://www.devo.com/bladerunner/
Includes links to an article titled 'Blade Runner riddle solved' and a posthumous interview with Philip K. Dick.